CONTAINER GARDENING
for Beginners

An Easy Guide to Grow Fresh Organic Vegetables and Ornamental Plants in Pots and Tiny Spaces

HANNAN ROSES

 *Copyright @ 2020 Hannah Roses - All rights reserved*

This book is written with the sole purpose of providing relevant information on a specific topic for which every reasonable effort has been made to ensure that it is both accurate and reasonable. Nevertheless, by purchasing this book you consent to the fact that the author, as well as the publisher, are in no way experts on the topics contained herein, regardless of any claims as such that may be made within. As such, any suggestions or recommendations that are made within are done so purely for entertainment value. It is recommended that you always consult a professional, prior to undertaking any of the advice or techniques discussed within.

This is a legally binding declaration that is considered both valid and fair by both the Committee of Publishers Association and the American Bar Association and should be considered as legally binding within the United States.

The reproduction, transmission, and duplication of any of the content found herein, including any specific or extended information will be done as an illegal act regardless of the end form the information ultimately takes. This includes copied versions of the work both physical, digital and audio unless express consent of the Publisher is provided beforehand. Any additional rights reserved.

Furthermore, the information that can be found within the pages described forthwith shall be considered both accurate and truthful when it comes to the recounting of facts. As such, any use, correct or incorrect, of the provided information will render the Publisher free of responsibility as to the actions taken outside of their direct purview. Regardless, there are zero scenarios where the original author or the Publisher can be deemed liable in any fashion for any damages or hardships that may result from any of the information discussed herein.

Additionally, the information in the following pages is intended only for informational purposes and should thus be thought of as universal. As befitting its nature, it is presented without assurance regarding its prolonged validity or interim quality. Trademarks that are mentioned are done without written consent and can in no way be considered an endorsement from the trademark holder.

Table of Contents

INTRODUCTION 5

CHAPTER ONE - The Best Potting Soil 9

CHAPTER TWO - Gardening Month By Month 17

    In the garden in January: what to plant, sow and do in January 18

    In the garden in February: what to plant, sow and do in February? 20

    In the garden in March: what to plant, sow and do in March? 23

    In the garden in April: what to plant, sow and do in April? 26

    In the garden in May: what to plant, sow and do in May? . 29

    In the garden in June: what to plant, sow and do in June? 32

    In the garden in July: what to plant, sow and do in July? ..35

    In the garden in August: what to plant, sow and do in August? 38

    In the garden in September: what to plant, sow and do in September? 40

    In the garden in October: what to plant, sow and do in October? 43

    In the garden in November: what to plant, sow and do in November? 46

    In the garden in December: what to plant, sow and do in December? 48

CHAPTER THREE - The Right Pot for Every Plant 51
CHAPTER FOUR - Recycled Pots 63
CHAPTER FIVE - Container Gardening Plan 73
CHAPTER SIX - Fruit and Vegetables in Pots 81
CHAPTER SEVEN - Vertical Planting System 97
   Vertical Gardening With Vegetables 106
   Vertical Gardening With Herbs 109
CHAPTER EIGHT - Raised Bed Gardening 113
   Advantages of Raised Beds Gardening 117
CONCLUSION 121

INTRODUCTION

Container gardening is a trendy new trend for people who may not have enough room for conventional gardening, or want to grow plants in a smaller space such as a patio or balcony. There are a few simple things to learn before beginning a container garden.

Although any container can be used for container gardening, water should be able to leave to prevent plants from getting too much water at any time. Place a small hole in the jar to remove excess water. You can go to a gardening store for a simple choice of wooden, ceramic or plastic garden pots. Many people enjoy using unique items from attics, antique shops, or even constructing their own. The sky is the limit and you can easily design your container garden.

Use good-quality soil after selecting the correct container. Choose a high-quality potting soil and select some fertilizer to help plants grow. Then choose where to put your garden. Sunlight is important since many plants require six or more hours of sunlight a day. Choose the best position for plant appearance and safety.

After gathering all supplies, pick your plants. For flowers year-round, start planting spring bulbs and then adding summer plants in June or July. Daffodils, tulips and hyacinths are perfect beauty options and hardy flowers. Some flower suggestions are iris, pansies, daisies, and crocuses. Choose your flowers based on the growing season. A perfect way to pick a color scheme is to look at flower catalogs and see what the bulbs are.

Growing plants in containers can be immensely rewarding and can be very therapeutic, like any planting. What could be better if you live in an apartment with a tiny balcony, than watching your pot plant garden or picking some fresh herbs or vegetables grown in containers and using them in your cooking.

Package gardens benefit from being portable. If you move home, you can take your garden with you, or just want a change and rearrange your plants. In a very short time, your garden will look fresh. A container garden is not the flat one dimension of a traditional garden but gives you the additional height dimension. By using pots of different heights, or putting them on tables, you will gain from several plant rates. It's nice to cover walls or untidy places. Your portable garden's design and the look is limited by ingenuity and imagination.

Being able to raise your container garden off the ground and ease of maintenance means these gardens are suitable for the elderly or wheelchair users, where falling to ground level and using heavy garden tools are not a choice. This is one of the most important advantages of potting plants and demonstrates how flexible it can be.

CHAPTER ONE
The Best Potting Soil

If you are thinking of planting in your garden or creating your own garden for plants, it is more than likely that you want to know which soil is best for plant growth. The type of soil and the quality varies, depending on where you are living, and even the soil in your garden does not have to be the same as that of your neighbor. The soil that is best for growing plants directly will be seen on the same plants that they grow.

Let's talk about outdoor and indoor soils so that you can see the differences between them and you can decide for yourself the best soil for the growth of plants.

Floors outside

Outdoor floors are usually of three different types:

- Of sand.
- Of clay.
- Slime or silt.

The ideal soil for most plants is one that is rich in nutrients, that is, sandy soil. But do not be overwhelmed if you think that your soil does not meet the appropriate conditions because you can always modify its conditions and make them optimal with a little fertilizer.

Indoor floors

If you have plants that are growing indoors, you may think it is a good idea to get the soil out into the garden for your plants to grow there, but this is a common mistake and also a bad idea.

Garden soil contains bacteria that can kill your houseplants. There's another option if you don't want to use the potting soil they sell in stores: sterilize the soil outside.

Sterilize the exterior floor

If you choose to decide that your indoor plants grow outdoors, you will have to sterilize the soil outside to eliminate diseases and get rid of insects and weeds. After sterilizing the soil, you will have to modify the soil with peat and sand, so your plants will have adequate drainage and the correct air so that there is good humidity.

You can also choose to buy commercial potting soil because they are very similar and more comfortable for you. These soils include peat moss and vermiculite; something that will cause a slow release of fertilizers suitable for the growth of your plants.

Both aspects will help your plants grow with strong roots because they will be able to obtain nutrients, humidity and adequate ventilation.

Know The Types Of Soil For Your Garden

To achieve a dream garden or have a well-kept corner of leafy plants, it is important that you know the types of soil, their characteristics and knows which one you need for each plant. The quality of the land is important!

Choosing the right substrate is also important for our crops to look good. Each type of soil has its particular physical and chemical characteristics, and in the market, you can get several types, but that will depend on the particular needs of your plant.

A substrate can make your plants more resistant to pests and other elements that can hinder their growth, as well as protect them from parasitic diseases.

Would you like to learn what you have about the land for cultivation and which ones are better suited to your plant type? Everything you're reading below is going to be very useful.

1. Prepared land

It is the ideal substrate for pots because they have good water drainage. In general, the prepared soil is the one used for the best growth of ornamental plants that you place in pots, planters, flower beds and gardens.

The prepared soil is the one recommended for the moment of sowing a new plant in a pot; this way, you can count on the assurance that its growth process will be optimal from the beginning.

This type of commercial land has a set of common components, among the most prominent of which are washed water, compost, moss and rice husk.

2. Professional land

This type of soil improves moisture retention and activates natural plant protection systems. It is a substrate that contains significant percentages of nitrogen, an ideal element for growing plants. The professional soil also has a mixture of black peat, peat moss, granules and perlite. When is it useful? Professional soil can be used in any crop, both indoors and outdoors.

Among the advantages of using this substrate is the fact that the plant will be healthier and stronger against diseases, thanks to its components. Another advantage of professional soil is that it is ideal for the root development of plants, in addition to contributing to more regular and uniform growth because the stems will be more robust.

In summary, when you buy professional soil, your plants can count on a better metabolism and a low incidence of diseases. This will mean larger, stronger and leafier plants.

3. Black Earth

Black soil tends to be very uniform and is recommended for grasses and pots. Black earth is distinguished precisely by its color (dark black) and its origin (it was formed after the decomposition of organic matter). Black earth is generally made up of remnants of dry leaves or organic waste. Of animals that are absorbed as nutrients by the soil.

This type of soil is very useful when making a crop or planting plants. It is widely used for the sowing of ornamental plants or also for the cultivation of plants that serve for our subsequent feeding. Black earth plays a fundamental role in these crops because it contains the necessary nutrients that promote the growth of flowers or fruits.

There are many benefits of black earth, but we can mention its natural capacity to retain enough water for the development of the plant. Also, its components are ideal for the circulation of the roots; in this way, the plant's growth is optimal and healthy.

4. Potting soil substrate

It is ideal for foliage, flowers and vegetables because it contains high levels of nutrients. The substrate is one of the best sources of food for plants, given that it has the capacity to grant fertility to the soil, as well as to provide the nutrients that the plant needs for its development to be as expected. Thanks to the substrate, various problems with plants that cause problems with their growth can be avoided.

Among the types of substrates, we can mainly highlight two types: organic substrates and inert substrates. Among the organic substrates, one of the most outstanding is earthworm humus, a type of substrate that provides greater fertility to the soil thanks to its particular composition: nitrogen, phosphorus, potassium, calcium, magnesium, iron and sodium, among other elements.

Furthermore, this substrate is capable of inhibiting the development of fungi and bacteria that can affect plants. Another of the best known organic substrates is mulch, a type of substrate that is responsible for preventing early erosion and that also provides a set of organic materials to the earth to protect it against high or low temperatures.

Coconut fiber, perlite, gravel and sand are in the group of inert substrates. This set of substrates has the ideal components to nourish plants, in addition to allowing good drainage of the soil and maintaining the correct humidity for its development.

5. Leafy ground

Leafy soil improves soil texture and allows better internal air passage. Leafy soil is considered the "black gold" of plants because it has the ability to provide a large number of nutrients (micronutrients and macronutrients).

You will notice its effects because your plants will be able to germinate better, their growth will be much faster, and their appearance will look stronger. By the time you decide to add leaf soil to your crops, you will be automatically improving the composition of the soil, as well as enriching it with various nutrients.

6. Organic land

Organic soil improves moisture retention and gives greater resistance to the plant. A great advantage is that it can be used on all types of plants. Organic soil is part of the fertilizer that should be given to plants in order to make their growth healthier.

Some expert gardeners use it as a garden filler because this type of soil has the ability to increase the number of nutrients in the soil.

7. Special lands

The special lands, due to their composition, are ideal in certain types of flowers such as orchids. These soils have the ability to provide the nutrients that floral plants need to make them look beautiful, with leafy leaves and brightly colored flowers.

Do you already know what type of land to choose? Beautifying a garden is more than just planting some plants and adding water from time to time. If you want healthy and strong ornamental plants, you have to look where you walk; yes, the lands are essential to achieve that goal. The diet of a plant and the absorption of nutrients will depend on the quality of the land you have purchased, and currently, all you need to know is the plant you have, in order to buy the right substrate.

Having a garden, land, plants and flowers in excellent conditions is not impossible; it begins by choosing the right soil and with the correct composition. Then everything will be easier: watch your little plant grow and grow stronger day by day.

If you are thinking of planting in your garden or creating your own garden for plants, it is more than likely that you want to know which soil is best for plant growth. The type of soil and the quality varies depending on where you are living, and even the soil in your garden does not have to be the same as that of your neighbor. The soil that is best for growing plants directly will be seen on the same plants that they grow.

CHAPTER TWO
Gardening Month By Month

In the greenhouse, the seasons punctuate the work from the vegetable garden to the orchard, going through the ornamental garden: the soil, like plants, needs rest periods until it flourishes again with spring's arrival.

The garden work evolves every month, from January to December, with periods more intensive than others: tillage, sowing, seeding, planting, harvesting ... Reminder sheets so that nothing can be missed or overlooked, and take good care of the fruits and vegetables that are grown. You'll also be exploring all the regular garden plays.

In the garden in January: what to plant, sow and do in January

January is clearly not the most favorable outdoor gardening month: frosts, wind, fog and snow are often brakes. Moreover, the vegetation is at rest; it takes time to start in spring again!

It's time to think about the layout of your garden, though, by redesigning it; for instance, in front of your desk, warm in front of a fireplace, with hot chocolate and some small chocolate hazelnuts madeleines!

Vegetable gardening in January: preparing the soil, planting and sowing

- The leek should be protected from excessive frost by a good layer of straw or leaves.
- Do a good plowing, incorporating the manure previously deposited in your soil.
- You can plant garlic and shallot bulbs. Under heated chassis, you will sow carrots. Under shelter, you can sow spring lettuces.
- Prepare the trenches for planting asparagus in the spring.
- It's time to check the expiration dates of your seeds and to clean your pea or row bean stakes with iron sulfate or bleach.

Gardening in the ornamental garden and flower beds in January

- In the ornamental garden, some flowering plants give colorful touches: Christmas roses, heather, camellias ... But, it will especially be necessary to prepare the garden for the end of winter. The Christmas party is over, and if you bought a Nordmann tree, for example, with roots, you need to replant it very quickly.
- First, plow the spaces that will receive annuals and claw the flowerbeds of biennials.
- Protect perennials from frost too intense with mulch, and clean by removing dried flowers and stems. Protect some shrubs that fear frost with a veil.
- Prepare the earthworks for your future lawn, if necessary. If you have a pool, break the ice that could have formed. Also, remember to feed small birds that suffer a little in winter!

In the garden in February: what to plant, sow and do in February?

February's weather is oddly close to January's, with the fact that the days get a little longer. It's common practice to say February is one of the coldest months ...

It is indeed the full winter sports season because there's snow! And either you're staying warm at home, dreaming and planning what you're going to do in your garden in the months ahead, or you're quitting your garden for a couple of days and going to the ski slopes for sports sliding!

Gardening in the vegetable patch in February

- Harvest the leeks and Brussels sprouts.
- Sow in a greenhouse or frame, carrots, summer leeks and lettuces. Plant the pink garlic and the claws of asparagus in the trenches prepared in January.
- Clean your strawberry planks: dry leaves and weeds. Divide the rhubarb feet.

Figure 1- hydrangeas

Gardening in the ornamental garden and flower beds in February

Figure 2- Azalea

- Plant the biennials if you haven't finished. There is still time to divide and replant the perennials. Plant rhododendrons and azaleas. Make your chrysanthemum cuttings and start sowing flower seeds for the summer.

- Clean hydrangeas by cutting dry branches.
- Prune roses and prune shrubs or vines that bloom on year-round wood.
- Devote yourself to your lawn, since there is little to do for the flowers: redraw its borders, air it, scarify it, sow it if you are at the creation stage!
- Take advantage of your first flowerings: crocuses, primroses, daffodils ...

In the garden in March: what to plant, sow and do in March?

Figure 3- tomato seedling

March's rains are typical of this crucial month, with bursts of heavy rain, snow, slush, and sleet between the end of winter and the beginning of spring. So far, don't hurry to the greenhouse, since relatively extreme colds can still occur: these March sleet only signal the spring's gradual arrival, so you can continue your greenhouse interventions more intensively.

The flowers are progressively growing, the winter defenses can be slowly eliminated, and according to the well-known adage, you will be able to indulge in the March sizes, considered the highest.

Gardening in the vegetable patch in March

- Seedlings of lettuce, chicory, broad beans, cabbage, spinach, turnips, parsnips, beets, radishes, celery, peas can be started, just like the leeks that you will transplant at the end of June for a fall-winter harvest after.
- If you have a warm mini greenhouse, the first sowing of tomatoes can be made. Aromatics such as basil, parsley, mint, rosemary, thyme, chives, will also be sown undercover.
- Potatoes can be planted after proper smoking.
- Also, pink plant garlic and white onion.
- If you have artichokes, take the most beautiful eyecups on the feet to transplant them and multiply the feet.

Gardening in the ornamental garden and flower beds in March

Seasonal flowers show up and start to brighten up the garden: primroses, serviceberry, Japanese quince, prunus, mimosa, and of course, the essential yellow forsythia heralding the arrival of spring!

- In the ornamental garden, remove and store the winter protections.
- Put compost at the foot of irises and peonies.

- Plant perennials as well as summer and fall flowering bulbs.
- Sow annuals, only under cover: petunias, verbena, sage, marigold, cosmos ...
- For shrubs, prune all hedges, as well as deflowering camellia, hibiscus, buddleia, wisteria ... Also, your last roses.
- Finish planting the deciduous bare-rooted shrubs and evergreen shrubs.
- Treat oleanders with Bordeaux mixture to avoid bacteriosis or pseudomonas, which manifests itself in black spots.

In the garden in April: what to plant, sow and do in April?

It's spring in April, but beware; the saying "Don't discover yourself by the thread in April" is still true! No hurry to expect too much sowing or planting at the risk of a late frost wiping out your efforts.

The world is slowly heating up, leaves and flower buds are bursting, but maintain defenses on the most vulnerable plant species as a precaution. Nothing is won yet, particularly since the reddish moon is conducive to night frosts during the lunation after Easter that makes young shoots russet.

Gardening in the vegetable patch in April

- Planting of melons, squash, carrots, cabbage, spinach, green beans, radishes, lettuce, beets, and other vegetables can begin.
- Plant early potatoes and leeks summer, along with rave celery and ribbed celery.
- You will need to thin the carrot seedlings made in March, leaving a plant every 4 to 5 cm.
- It's time to transplant lettuce plants.
- Divide the chives, sow the parsley.

- Prepare the ground where you will plant your tomatoes. Only regions with a mild climate will be able to start planting them during the second half of April.

The ornamental garden in April: flower beds, trees and shrubs

Spring is here with the blooming of all the bulbs hidden in the beds, lawns and tubs of terraces: tulips, hyacinths, daffodils, and muscaris. Perennial side, the silver basket is in bloom, like the asters and the heart of Mary. The periwinkles, the thoughts are resplendent, and the lilac scents. It is also the month of the syringe, the magnolia, the ceanothes, the azalea, the rhododendron, and the orange tree of Mexico.

- Sow the annual flowers directly in place: forecastle, California poppy, nasturtium, snapdragon, cosmos, and zinnia.
- Plant perennials in your beds.
- Plant the dahlias and the bulbs that will bloom in summer or fall (lilies, gladioli, cannas ...).
- It's time to prepare the balconies and terraces planters that you will garnish with summer flowers.
- Repot the oleanders in containers, which need them.

- As time goes by, remove the wilted flowers from the daffodils, hyacinths and tulips without touching the leaves or bulbs.
- There is no emergency going to buy your summer flowers in a garden center, even if it is tempting!
- Prune the spring flowering shrubs at the end of it.
- Cut the hydrangeas and lay the wisteria.
- Plant conifers, as well as shrubs and roses in containers. Hoe at the foot and mulch them.
- Make your first hedge pruning.

Other small interventions in April

- At home, repot your green plants, which are a bit cramped.
- Make the first mowing of the grass and scarify if necessary.

In the garden in May: what to plant, sow and do in May?

In May, valley lily opens the month with May 1st tradition! It's the peak of spring: all the plants burst and expand noticeably, with the wonderful days. A tiny field; look out for the Ice Saints: a late jelly can be fatal for some plants or for some shrubs!

The flowers give color and fragrance symphony: anemones, imperial fritillaries, columbines, bellflowers, Mary's heart, iris, lupins, peonies ... Without overlooking the flowering of shrubs such as laburnum, ceanothe, deutzia, magnolia, tamarisk, Judas vine, and much more, including the famous and beautiful lilac!

Gardening in the vegetable patch in May: planting, sowing, harvesting

- Sowing in the open ground of chives, carrots, turnips, fennel, pumpkins, parsley, lettuce, beans, tetragon can be undertaken,
- The cauliflower and autumn cabbage will be transplanted,
- The feet of tomatoes can be placed everywhere in the ground, as well as eggplants, melons, peppers and basil,

- The radish and asparagus harvest is at its maximum. Do not forget to sow radishes every ten days in order to have a staggered harvest,
- Harvest the salads,
- The chicory seedlings that will make your endives next winter are to be done now.

The ornamental garden in May: flower beds, trees and shrubs

- All summer flowers can now be placed in the ground (or in planters) including geraniums,
- You can still do annual sowing in place, including climbers (nasturtium, bohemian, sweet pea, ...),
- Plant lilies of the valley in the shade,
- If you have a pond, you can plant water lilies and pond plants there
- Cut the stems of perennials that are deflowered (iris, aubrietes ...) without touching the leaves,
- Crop roses, remove gourmets of roses, suckers of lilac and hazelnut,
- Tear off the deflowered spring bulbs and continue planting the summer bulbs,

- Take out the cacti and succulents as well as the plants in the tub (oleander ...).
- Prune spring-flowering shrubs as well as coniferous hedges,
- Plant ornamental shrubs bought in containers,
- Prune the heather that has finished flowering,
- Make hydrangea cuttings!

Other small interventions in May

- At home, during the second half of the month, gradually bring out the plants which are hardy enough to spend the summer outside on the terrace,
- If you have a veranda or a greenhouse, ventilate it well during the day,
- Lawn mowing should now be weekly,
- Watch for powdery mildew, aphids, slugs, rust, etc.
- Do your maintenance work on floors, fences, low walls, and underground watering.

In the garden in June: what to plant, sow and do in June?

"In June, if it rains, feed your fist" Oh? Funny comment, but what of a prologue! Fortunately, the saying library seems to find a great source of inspiration in June, and something more inspiring must be included ... "Beautiful sunshine that comes in June has never ruined anybody." That's better, and what could be more true?

June is the month with all dreams, marking the end with spring and the beginning of summer. The sun begins becoming a frequent resident; the first tanning marks emerge, indicating long lazing sessions on the beach. But we're not there yet (a little abrupt back to reality, but let's not hide anything, all these beautiful images are there only for the poetic side). Let's then go back to our goats. Holiday time hasn't come yet, much less for the gardener who won't get bored in the coming month.

The vegetable garden in June

Weeding, hoeing, watering. There will be no shortage of activities this month in the vegetable patch. No matter what happens, weeding and hoeing are essential so that weeds do not encroach on the vital space of your vegetables.

Watering will depend more on the season and on the plant, of course. If the weather is not too dry, settle for a punctual watering, preferably in the evening. Seedlings must, however, benefit from daily watering to get up well (again, prefer to water in the evening so that all the water does not evaporate).

Other activities are also required during the month of June for many vegetables:

- Butter: peas, beans, potatoes (already start to prevent the risk of downy mildew)
- Prune: tomatoes, melons
- Stake: cucumbers, pickles
- Lighten: carrots, lettuce, beets, turnips
- Sow: Brussels sprouts, autumn cauliflower, chard, squash
- Transplant: leeks,
- Harvest: garlic, shallots, onions, early potatoes, spinach, carrots

In addition to seasonal activity, we must also think about the future and start preparing for the next harvest by sowing certain vegetable plants. You can also sow strawberries for future seasons.

The ornamental garden in June

The ornamental garden also generates its share of activities. Sow the last annuals in the beds. Butte the gladioli, mulch the dahlias, plant the fall bulbs (Naples cyclamen, crocuses, crocus ...). Sow poppies in the field and hollyhocks in the nursery.

Remember to regularly remove faded flowers to avoid the rise in seeds and to promote flowering.

For the cuttings, divide the spring perennials after flowering: delphinium, lupine, népéta ...

Weed the beds, water and mulch and then mow the lawn regularly!

In the garden in July: what to plant, sow and do in July?

"Everyone who sleeps until the rising sun in July will inevitably die late" ... And the proverb is true. The month of July marks the beginning of the summer, the holidays, the long relaxing hours in the pool hammock. But as jovial and fun as they may be, all these things should not make you forget the life of your vegetable garden, which will inevitably perish if you abandon it on such a good road.

July is the month of performance, and it is during this period that the fruit of your efforts begins to become truly concrete! But who says yield in such a small room tells lots of tenants. No major work in July but a multitude of small "household" tasks to keep your garden balanced.

The vegetable garden in July

IN July, the vegetable garden is an authentic Spanish inn. All kinds of vegetables coexist; some depart, some arrive, and some are on the way. Therefore this month is going to be the month of repairs, and we're going to have to handle this whole little universe and make sure everybody has everything they need. Daily hoeing is needed for most of them because the weeds that landed in the garden since June are not ready to decamp without a little hoe in the back. You should also remember to water regularly, preferably at night, to prevent the water from evaporating and to take care not to wet the leaves to prevent disease. Also, scrape the surface to crack the crust to make it easier for the water to penetrate.

- Butter: potatoes, beans (as soon as the first leaves are well developed).
- Prune: cucumbers, zucchini, tomatoes.
- Sowing: carrots and radishes (always sowing every two weeks for a regular harvest), lettuces, cabbage, turnips.
- Also, take advantage of an empty garden plot to sow your green manure.

The ornamental garden in July

The ornamental garden is probably the most affected part of your yard, as the flowers aren't able to bear the heat well. Who has never returned from holidays to discover a mass of completely desiccated plants with dread? Therefore, you must help your flowers survive the stormy heat that is suffocating them by watering regularly in July (watering is not required every day either). Start by cleaning your beds and hoeing, and weeding your soil, so the water penetrates well. Again, watering in the evening is easier, but also monitoring the forecast to make sure it doesn't rain the next day. The plants are definitely thirsty, but that isn't an excuse to drown them.

The time has come to tutor your dahlias and your gladioli to help them not to bow under the force of the stormy winds of July.

If you go on vacation, remember to cut all the flowers of your roses and other flowering shrubs to benefit from a new flowering on the return.

For many plants, July is the month of multiplication:

- Cuttings: hydrangeas
- Tuft division: primroses and irises
- Harvesting of seeds: wallflowers, lupins, columbines and poppies
- Harvest of spring bulbs

In the garden in August: what to plant, sow and do in August?

"Even though you like the diaper, don't sleep under the light of August." These words are really wise. Indeed, it's hardly advised to indulge in a nap under the hot rays of August unless you want to obey some fashion calling to go red from head to toe. And this heat is possibly what drives most French citizens to go on holiday this month. Just here, if you're happy to go far away and forget about work and trouble, the garden remains there and continues to claim its regular maintenance.

The vegetable garden in August

As with gardening in July, the garden is often full in August, and there is no shortage of work. Most of the vegetables are at the end of their growth and are preparing to leave the vegetable garden, so you have to watch out for the "final adjustments," which could hinder the final maturation phase. If you've brought green manures to high-yielding vegetables, such as beans orchard, which tend to rob the soil of its nutrients, they will do very well.

- Transplant: seedlings from the previous month such as leeks, lettuce, cabbage.
- Sow: winter or late vegetables such as carrots, radishes, turnips or lamb's lettuce.

- Harvest: the potatoes which must be left to dry for a while before returning them.
- Multiply: division of rhubarb tufts by cutting them off using a tool like a spade.

The ornamental garden in August

The ornamental garden requires a lot of work in August. Some plants such as hollyhocks, amaranths, dahlias and gladioli grow and are more fragile in the wind, so they must be staked.

It is also necessary to prune wilted flowers such as daylilies, cosmos and lupins.

Transplant the biennials, like the wallflowers, which have reached a satisfactory size. Transplant, preferably in the evening. For a few days, it will be necessary to water a little more abundantly than usual.

Continue to water regularly if the weather is too dry so that the plants do not wilt. If you go on a trip, abundantly water the base of your plants so that they have a good supply of water.

If you want to dry some of your flowers (hydrangeas, for example), it's time to pick them, and hang them upside down in your basement or cellar.

Finally, make sure that ants and aphids do not invade the territory.

In the garden in September: what to plant, sow and do in September?

"Buy wood and clothes in September!" While the weather is still mild and sunny, winter is not far away, and we'll have to start preparing ourselves for the cold December and other months of not so warm temperatures at home and in the garden! Of course, without forgetting (to start in the good news), that September is the month of the school year's starting. No more hours of sun rest, and early nap on the terrace lunch. Give way to screaming alarm clocks at midnight, hours lost in traffic congestion, and dishes with a more than dubious presence in the canteen.

The vegetable garden in September

The vegetable garden likes the September month (obviously it is not he who comes back to work the guy!). The soil is perfect, though retaining last summer's heat; it also finds the autumn nights' humidity that gives the garden's soil a real renewal. September brings the end of summer with it, and at the end of the season, the gardener will have to enjoy his last tomatoes and other vegetables while a great maintenance job awaits him.

- Transplant: curly chicory and escarole under a forcing veil
- Sow: lamb's lettuce, chervil, onions, spinach, leeks and radishes. Also, sow parsley in pots for the winter.

- Plant: strawberries! A small ray of sunshine this September; strawberries love the warm and humid soil of this end of season.
- Harvest: all the root vegetables, the potatoes (continuing to let them dry on the spot before bringing them in), the rhubarb petioles, and the last tomatoes that you can let ripen in the sun.

The ornamental garden in September

The ornamental garden shows itself to be much less sympathetic and loads you with its lot of work. As for the previous month, you must regularly remove the faded flowers from your beds, especially dahlias, to obtain future vigorous flowers.

Fold-down the flower stalks of hollyhocks and give all the roses organic fertilizer.

It is now time to plant the bulbs collected last spring. The daffodil bulbs must be loosened every other year.

Also sow poppies (to get flowers next spring), as well as chrysanthemums.

Transplant the biennials that have reached a satisfactory size.

For those who did not have time to go about it in August, there is still time to cut roses, fuchsias and geraniums. Divide tufts of peonies.

Harvest the seeds of nasturtiums, marigolds, carnations, lupins and moths. Before enclosing the seeds in a container (preferably opaque), allow them to air dry to prevent moisture from causing them to rot.

In the garden in October: what to plant, sow and do in October?

Indeed, the gardener will still not be able to rest on the garden side this month. It might just as well be a concession for those who were always hoping for a potential time-out: this would never happen. Under the Elbow, the garden will still have an occupation to confuse you. Yet, essentially, admit it, you like it. What would the gardener have been without a small hoe corner, a repot plant or a prune tree? It's to prevent such a sense of uselessness that the October month gives him his share of the toil. This work will consist mainly of last harvests and field preparation for the cold season.

The vegetable garden in October

During this time, life in the vegetable garden was relatively calm, and the plots were slowly cleared. It's time to get the vegetables harvested and stored in a dry place to protect them. Take your vegetables in the morning to keep them from rotting from the moisture, then let them dry all day. Among other items, the last pumpkins can be harvested with delicacy (shocks threaten to hurt them), then placed on a straw pad. Store the carrots, turnips, beets and black radishes at the end of the month. Store them between two layers of sand in the night.

Sowing black radishes are always possible, but they will have to be placed under a frame so that they do not die of cold.

You can also plant garlic and shallots.

Celery must be tied to make it blanch.

The onions from early August must be transplanted.

The ornamental garden in October

Just as the ornamental garden is the one that suffers the most from the heat, it is also the one that suffers the most from harsh winters. So we will have to prepare all these little people so that they can survive without too much trouble.

This involves taking in overly chilly plants such as orchids, hibiscus and most green plants.

Geraniums and oleanders should be placed in a cool, well-ventilated area. Take the opportunity to cut them to 10cm.

Also, bring in citrus fruits.

Remove the annual plants that are wilting, and cut the flower stalks of the hollyhocks, and the wilted flowers of the crocosmias.

The dahlias are fragile and could bend under the slightly more violent winds of autumn. It is, therefore, more prudent to tutor them.

You can now plant the spring bulbs in-depth, covering them with a protective layer, like peat.

Divide and replant perennials, as well as roses. Mulch the soil to protect the roots.

In the garden in November: what to plant, sow and do in November?

November's month is a rainy month: the late fall rain but not drier in winter. You'll harvest your last crops, and start growing frost-fearing plants. It is particularly the time of planting your trees and shrubs because, as a popular saying goes, "At Sainte Catherine, all wood takes root!."

The vegetable garden in November

Harvest the last root vegetables and pick the Brussels sprouts. Protect the winter cabbage and butte the artichokes that you can mulch more to protect them from frost.

Drain the garden hoses, especially those that are buried, and reinsert the garden hoses. Disinfect all guardians before returning them.

Empty your compost bin so you can put new leaves in it. And if you have a greenhouse, it's time to clean the windows.

The ornamental garden in November

For perennials, cleaning the beds is essential: remove all dry flowers and stems. Regarding chrysanthemums, do the same at the end of the month only. Divide the feet of some perennials and replant immediately.

Plant the gladioli, dahlias and cannas, and let them dry in the dry before storing them undercover.

Plant biennials and spring-flowering bulbs. Plant camellias and roses. Prune summer or fall flowering shrubs.

At the beginning of the month, it's time to do the last mowing of the lawn. Then clean, sharpen and wipe the blade of your mower, which you will store until the following year. Regularly rake the leaves that fall on your lawn.

If you have a pond, remove the fallen leaves from it to prevent them from rotting or protect your pond with a tarpaulin.

In the garden in December: what to plant, sow and do in December?

While December's month is not very favorable for the garden, some tasks can still be carried out. For starters, planting a few trees and shrubs would be possible, and growing a certain number of vegetables such as cabbage, or even applying a ground fertilizer to your soils, if they are not frozen.

Flowers

- Plant your new roses
- Weed and properly clean your flower beds

Vegetables

- Pull out dead annuals and biennials
- Harvest beets, carrots, cabbage, leeks, salsify …

Fruits

- Plant your fruit trees
- Prune and prune if necessary

Trees and shrubs

- Plant your ornamental trees and shrubs
- Compost the last leaves, clean
- Remove the moss from the trees with a brush and/or brush them with lime

General maintenance

- Cover your surfaces if the ground is not frozen
- Amend if necessary

CHAPTER THREE
The Right Pot for Every Plant

Far from being a secondary aspect, they are a crucial element for the development of a plant. Something that forces us to know a little more in-depth about the types of pots that exist and what are their different applications. The way to get it right when we choose it; and make our plant not only look prettier than it is, but above all, grow with health and well-being.

A pot or planter is not just the container in which we have a plant. It is also their home and their natural way of life. Two compelling reasons why, beyond aesthetic questions, we choose a pot according to the specific needs of a plant.

Types Of Pots: Interior Or Exterior?

At first glance, we can believe that a pot is still a pot and that it is perfect for any space. However, the types of indoor and outdoor pots vary substantially in the same way that the specific requirements of plants vary from one environment to another.

For starters, if we have to choose pots for outdoor plants, we will have to consider some fundamental needs:

- Choosing a pot with the guarantee of correct drainage: especially for pots located in gardens or terraces and without a roof that covers them, it is essential to carefully review this topic. Keep in mind that in the pots exposed to rain, we cannot control the amount of watering, so being able to evacuate any excess is vital to prevent the roots of the plant from rotting. Sometimes the drainage holes are marked in the pot itself so that we can make them according to the use we are going to give them.

The clay pots allow the perspiration and evaporation of the water.

- Choosing a material resistant to frost and UV rays from the sun: reviewing this aspect will guarantee that in moments of extreme temperature, both upward and downward, the pots will maintain their original state and function! In this last aspect, both fiberglass and plastic

are ideal. We will always have to avoid metal and glass pots, which can break with changes in temperature.
- Choose pots that facilitate transportation: if we contemplate large plants in our garden or terrace, such as palm trees or fruit trees, we will have to choose pots that allow us to attach wheels to be able to move them easily.

When choosing between the types of pots when it comes to indoor plants, we will have fewer demands:

- Any material is suitable for indoor pots: something that includes both glass and metal since the temperatures inside a house are always more stable and balanced.
- Opting for these types of pots will allow us to save up to 40% of water.

Opt for self -watering pots: a perfect option for the maintenance of indoor plants but also to minimize cleaning around them. This type of pot has a specific tank for water, which will facilitate the irrigation work for plants that live in environments where there is environmental dryness.

Types Of Pots Specific To Some Plants

Besides knowing the final location of a plant before choosing between the various types of pots, telling us if you have particular needs is also important. Furthermore, there are plants that demand different pots, either by arranging their roots or by their needs for growth. When purchasing plants, this is something that never hurts to learn in order to give the plant just what it wants.

And, while the aim is to find out about each plant, let's know some that will need special pots:

Bonsai pots

Since we all know that growing a bonsai is an art, the focus is not only on the plant's main product in this case, but also on the environment that makes the central thing look even better. You should know pot is not just a bonsai frame; it's part of the whole thing.

Figure 4 - Bonsai

There are several types of pots with bonsai. The most popular are ceramic bonsai pots and mica bonsai pots, which can be found in a variety of shapes: rectangular, oval, rounded, octagonal, dished and probably the best-looking separate pot of water. The best pots are all made by hand and made according to the ancient Chinese norms. You should also be aware of the fact that the color of the leaves changes when choosing the right color for your pot, and so makes the visual connection between pot and tree.

So, in winter months, what looks good may not look appealing. Regular width or diameter of a pot should be close to the area the branches take. This does not apply entirely to pots on water-land where pots should be wider. Water-land pots are the rarest but potentially the best-looking dishes. These pots are split in the center and filled with soil on one side and water on the other.

Because of their shallow root systems, tray-type pots are ideal for both bonsai care and small cacti. The ideal container so that the roots of both of them can grow in width as they need.

Pots for succulent plants

It doesn't sound like much, but choosing the right pot to grow succulents is of utmost importance. You can greatly facilitate the care of these beautiful plants.

Succulent plants generally referred to as succulents derive their name from the thickness and fleshiness of their base, leaves and roots. This particularity is due to the unique type of fabric that composes them, the aquifer parenchyma, which has the capacity to absorb the little water available in the regions of origin. It is acting as a reservoir, and releasing water when needed, during long periods of drought typical of arid and dry places where succulents have adapted to live.

There are thousands of species, divided into various botanical families, in form, scale and colors, but all very original and exotic, varying much from one another. Even the shape has been determined for survival in nature, and in fact, these plants take on the strangest square, oval, and rosette shapes, and the proportions are usually reduced to a minimum to minimize respiration and suddenness. Some species have turned the leaves into thorns, conferring chlorophyll function on the plant.

- *Points to consider when choosing succulent pots*

The right pot can highlight the natural beauty of any succulent; even so, never buy a pot just for being beautiful.

First, make sure the pot has drainage holes. If they do not have them, the pot will retain the water, and the plant will rot.

On the other hand, some pots have holes, but they are small. When growing succulents, look for pots with the largest holes.

Prevent the substrate from being lost through the drainage using a maya that allows water to pass through but retains the soil.

Second, choose a pot that is slightly larger than the succulents. If the container is too large, it will retain too much water, and the plant will die.

- *What are the best succulent pots*

Every succulent collector really enjoys buying pots. There are countless options for colors, textures, patterns, shapes and sizes on the market. Let's talk a little bit about the types of succulent pots on the market.

1. Clay pots

The best option for beginners in the world of succulents is clay pots. Clay or clay pots are made from raw soil and have many benefits for plants.

They are air permeable. That means that the soil and roots can breathe. This will be healthier for the plant if it remains in an environment where it does not receive much airflow.

Another advantage is that clay pots remove excess moisture. I guess its biggest downside is that they are easy to break if they fall off.

2. Ceramic flower pots

Ceramic flower pots have the same benefits as clay flower pots. The problem with many is that they don't have drainage holes. Bottom holes can be drilled with a drill and glass drill. The process requires patience and practice.

Another option is to leave the succulent in the propagation pot and place it in a slightly larger second ceramic pot. When you water your plants, it will be necessary to remove them from the ceramic container.

3. Concrete pots

The pot's concrete is modern and clean. They are an excellent choice for succulent plants. Like ceramic pots, many sell them without a drain hole.

4. Plastic flower pots

Succulents can be grown in plastic pots with no problem. Of course, you must be very careful with irrigation because they tend to retain moisture.

The best thing about plastic pots is how colorful they are and how many options are on the market. Another benefit is that they are lightweight.

One downside is that the plastic pots are roasted in the sun. Be sure to buy thick pots. These will last longer.

5. Wooden flower pots

Wooden flower pots are becoming more and more fashionable. It gives a rustic style to any arrangement with succulents.

Wood pots work very well because it keeps the soil cool when the succulents are placed in the sun. What I don't know is how long these pots will last exposed to the elements before they rot.

6. Glass pots or terrariums

Despite the fact that succulents look beautiful in glass containers, I do not recommend their use.

Glass is not permeable to water and air. This will create evaporation and drainage problems. I am not saying that it is impossible to grow succulents in glass, but you have to be very careful with watering and where the arrangement is placed.

- *How to find the right size*

The most common mistake when growing succulents is planting them in pots too big for the size of the plant. Just pick pots a few inches wider than the succulent's circumference.

Suppose you have a succulent that is 3 centimeters wide. In this case, choose a pot with a diameter of 5 to 6 centimeters.

- *How to choose pots for succulents most suitable*

In choosing the most suitable succulent plant pots, it is necessary to consider the size of the plant and the type of roots; only the multiple and tangled ones adapt to each pot, but more often than not, it is advisable to choose a rather tall pot, and also considering the layer drainage that must be created on the bottom.

The pot should not be too small, even if the succulent plants tolerate them more than others; nor too large, because this means more land and, therefore, more water retained. Succulents fear above all, excess humidity. Therefore the most suitable material for pots for succulents is the earthenware, which, as mentioned, allows the soil to breathe. It is also possible to use a saucer in which to place sand or earth to be wet instead of soil, so that the pot absorbs the little moisture from the substrate and transmits it to the plant therefore, in a constant way.

Plastic pots are generally not suitable for succulents, especially black ones, given that they retain heat and transmit it to the plant, which can favor parasites and fungi.

CHAPTER FOUR
Recycled Pots

Anything that is made from recycled materials is welcome in The Green Blog, and that is why we are going to show you next, some nice recycled pots for the garden and with which you can plant all kinds of plants in addition to having your own fully decorated garden.

Recycled pots allow us to find an application for articles we may have thrown at home that is unhelpful. It is possible to fill the balconies, gardens or patios with color and originality from the pots that can be made from items like a bottle of wine, milk cartons and even old CDs or floppy disks that are no longer used.

All the materials that you will see below, not only do we surely have them at home, but they are also easily cleaned, and we can handle them without problems.

When it comes to making flower pots with recycled material, there are as many ways to do it as you can think of ideas. In the end, it's about looking at that container you were going to throw away, letting the light bulb light up, and by the time you want to realize it, you already have something new and original.

Of course, always be careful with the tools and materials used so that they are not dangerous or cause accidents.

Recycled flowerpots with plastic bottles, cans and pallets, but surely once you get into them, you can think of many more ways to make your own designs.

Original Garden Pots

If we were to tell you about the best materials for the manufacture of recycled pots, then the metal will definitely be the leader of our ranking, and we could get it from soda cans. If you choose preserves to make pots, remember to put a thick plastic inside so that the water doesn't oxidize it.

Plastic is also a good material for making recycled pots, and it must also be said to be cheaper but more "hard" when handling items such as containers or bottles.

Glass is another recommended item to make your pots recycled for the garden, but it's more complicated than it is because we have to make holes to drain the plant. If we want to make them, we'll need a thread soaked in alcohol and a glass drill bit. In general, glass is used as a pot with plants growing in water, such as a pot.

Tretrapac boxes are also recycled materials that can be used for our pots. They work well, clean quickly and do not require additional elements.

As far as "unconventional" materials and objects are concerned, we can always take advantage of computer parts, toys, kitchen containers and even unused shoes.

We can already begin to see what kind of materials we have at home and make our recycled pots! Remember, it's a good idea to use apple cider vinegar to clean them.

Flower Pots With Plastic Bottles

As we can see, people's creativity is boundless and can concentrate on reuse items that allow for a reduction in waste production and environmental protection. We stated earlier that plastic is material for recycled pots. The plastic bottles can be quickly obtained and turned into a pot quite quickly.

Others have even made big plastic bottles of gardens. The positive thing is that we can create or even manufacture hanging pots in different sizes and shapes. In the picture below, you can find an example of a garden with the most convenient plastic bottles. You can find the following.

Flower Pots With Glass Bottles

The bottles can be recycled and made in various varieties. Many pots made of plastic bottles have already been seen, but you can do real wonders by using glass bottles. If not, check out this beautiful oval floral pot made of glass bottles. The truth is, this pot looks like a true professionals' job already and can be found in a small square in a neighborhood. The question is: How many bottles does the pot manufacturer have to use (nearly 300, I say)?

You also have far simpler possibilities to turn a glass bottle into a pot if you do not want to go into a "run" of the previous caliber.

There is no brand we want to endorse, but it's as easy as using a soda bottle.

You do not need to use bottles. Specifically, you can turn any glass container in your house into pots. For example, the use of typical preserves or jam jars is very common.

Pots With Yogurt Containers

Because we are talking about pots that are recycled, the Yogurt jar you have completed can also be used. Don't just throw them down! Don't throw them away! They can serve as a flowerpot when they are big.

Our idea is to convert the liter Yogurt containers into pots, using spray paints or applying templates to beautify your creation. Let the varnish or embroidery you have made dry; fill them with dirt and voila! You can use them, for example, for small spices to always have on hand in the kitchen.

Flower Pots With Books

This other idea is very original, and if you love books, which are really beautiful objects, their use is really fascinating. Obviously, you should have some fat books that you do not want, in order to turn them into a flower pot and then place it on a piece of furniture, perhaps on your desk or on your nightstand. It could also be a great gift idea!

To create this beautiful pot, you must cut a sufficient number of pages to be able to insert, for example, a small fat plant (perfect for this type of container because it requires little care and especially little water); and place a plastic sheet around the Space cut to prevent water and dirt from ruining the rest of the book.

Flower Pot With A Wooden Box

Making a flower pot with a wooden box is a simple procedure that provides a significant and natural product. With their impressive size, these containers can hold more than one floor: what would you use to transform your courtyard into a small plant garden, where fresh crops and spices are planted, or even a certain amount of salads are planted, or to produce colorful floral work on a patio or garden?

The wooden boxes are perfect for growing plants, and you only need a few tips: hand primer specifically in order to protect the wood from the sun and rain, and ensure that water can flow underneath by a small opening, if not present, to prevent stagnation inside the pot.

Flower Pots With Concrete Or Cement

Cement pots are very modern and very original. All of us can produce a highly elegant and very natural outcome. Use old food containers in plastic or carton, like molds, to give your designs the most diverse forms; a mix of one piece of cement and four parts of sand are enough.

Fill a jar with the mix, leave a hole and allow to dry for a few days. Eventually, you should have some holes with the drainage boiler. You fill the earth and voila in the vacuum! You can begin putting your plants now.

Flower Pots With Pallets

If you have a small terrace and you have used up space on the street, it's time to think about rising upwards. Nothing like wagering on the most famous recycled pots of all for this. The pallet planters with which you can cultivate several varieties of plants without having to occupy huge sizes.

Fix the pallet if it is damaged and add a wooden or cloth panel corresponding to the part of the structure that rests on the wall; then choose the quality of the plants that can be flowering plants or some vegetable varieties like cucumber or peppers and position them in the platform's natural holes. If you opt for waterfall-growing plants, the effect will be very good, the pallet will hardly be noticed and you will get a real green wall.

Pots With Coffee Bags

If you are not a big fan of traditional flower pots, these recycled flower pots are ideal for you. We suggest that you make pots with jute bags, among which those of coffee or rice are perfect; you will get really original and absolutely cheap pots. Also, you will bet for care to the environment as these bags are made from materials completely recycled and biodegradable.

To accomplish that, you just have to fill your sacks with some soil and plant your flowers or aromatic herbs or even fat seedlings; these creations give your terrace a natural feel or wherever you want to put them.

Flower Pots With Cans

If you have creative skills, by painting old cans with paint, you can choose to make your own recycled pots, which are great because they have a smooth surface. You can draw what you want, adding rhinestones or beads with soft or vivid colors; there is no limit to the imagination!

It is also possible to stick colored or pre-printed fabrics around the jars or to use the newspapers that we saw before; the only precaution during construction is to drill the drainage holes before adding soil and seedlings.

More Recycled Garden Pots

There are also those who are looking for other more original and fun solutions. For example, do you remember those wellies (or katiuskas) that you used to wear and that you never wear anymore, because they are too small for you or you have moved to an area where they are not necessary? Well, you can also turn your wellies into fun garden pots. As data, you could even paint them to make them even more beautiful.

Following clothing, others decide to turn their pants into garden pots. The truth is that they give a slightly strange impression, but it is a good way to reuse clothes that we no longer use.

Toy Animals

How many times do we get rid of toys because children get tired of them; that's why when they reach adolescence, they only have a few soft toys left on the shelf and, at most, a box with their favorites, well kept in the back of the closet.

This time before deciding what to do with them, consider giving them another use. See what more original plant pots can be made by recycling some toy animals. You just need to give it a touch of color, make a hole in the top and place the plant that you like the most. The best, succulent, which is tiny and does not require much water.

Bicycle

This idea is classic, surely we have all seen it before, but it is so beautiful and romantic that I wanted to uncover it. I like it like that; rusty, but also painted yellow from top to bottom; white, in the middle of the garden, leaning against a tree or even hanging on the wall, it doesn't matter; it always looks great! Grab that grungy old bike and dust it off, then fill it with pots. Put one in the front basket part; if you have never had a basket, then great, because its time has come. Change the saddle for a plant that you love and fill the wheels with more and more flowers?

Tires

At Handfie, we love to recycle old tires and make things with them, in this case, a very cool pot for our aloe vera? To create it, join a pair of tires, paint them in color you like best and place a geotextile mesh inside, all you have to do is choose the plant that you like the most.

CHAPTER FIVE
Container Gardening Plan

For many people, container gardening has become the primary go-to method of gardening, particularly for people with different physical abilities. Gardening in containers is highly adaptable and can be achieved in a way that makes the entire wider garden experience ready and waiting for anyone, even if they're in a wheelchair. They're not as big as they used to be, or have certain physical disabilities that make conventional gardening difficult.

Not only activity in the garden needs to be considered, but convenient access for simple enjoyment also needs to be considered for residents and disabled people who may not enjoy working in a garden but enjoy spending time in the garden. Container gardening makes most physical disabilities a non-issue and opens the hobby to green thumbs and brown thumbs alike.

Container garden preparation requires flexibility, so it works for everyone involved. Simultaneously, space must be beautiful and well-designed as a coherent landscape. Adhering to traditional garden design and building up usable beds is a good technique, and is simple to do.

When constructing custom raised beds and containers, think about how people can move and operate with plants in them if they are in wheelchairs or walkers. Containers must be mounted in an area providing complete access to the entire container from at least the front and sides. Beds should not be too large and sprawling to fatigue and confuse people. Also, for those who are not physically strong, not a burden, containers and raised beds must be a treat. Starting too big can be more like work and drudgery, not an exuberant day out in the garden and enjoying the day.

Using an already formulated soil mix is good practice. Typically, these blends are free of harmful species that can make people sick. They are usually sold in conveniently portable sizes, making adding soil to raised beds simpler. And, it's usually priced dry and not so hard. A fine, high-quality mix also grows plants well.

Fertilizer is preferred. If you intend to follow the dosing directions on drug bags, don't be afraid. Plants grown in containers need plenty of food, particularly plants growing edible harvests like tomatoes and lettuces.

Pest management isn't as simple as soil preparation and fertilization choices. It's not a smart idea to put chemicals into a position where people have poor immune systems and sensitivities that healthy people don't have to think about. Prepare using hands to patch bugs as you see them, or manually delete damaged leaves and stems. Make a gentle insecticide soap to kill indoor bugs like spider mites, aphids, and other common indoor pets. Insecticidal soap can also work well outdoors. Often a sick plant can literally need to be discarded, not trifled.

When picking a container, make sure the gap is not too small because it's hard to plant in. Stop using inferior plastic containers. Glazed ceramic pots are a decent choice, but should have enough holes to drain water. Most wooden containers can rot. Exceptions are cedar and redwood containers.

Use very small containers because they keep plant roots from spreading. When planting deep root vegetables, go into deep containers. Also, consider how many plants you want to grow in the jar. Containers should have appropriate drainage holes. Every hole should be at least half an inch in diameter. Cover the pot base with a newspaper so that the soil does not spill from the drainage holes.

If you live in an area with high year-round temperatures, choose light color containers to absorb less heat. Excessive heat absorption leads to root growth. If you want to use clay pots, note that clay doesn't hold moisture well. Check the pots from time to time, so the plants have enough moisture.

Soilless mixtures work best for container gardens. They drain easily, are light in weight, and contain no weeds and pests. Buy these potting mixtures from your nearest nursery. Whenever you put soil in a jar, leave about two inches from the top. This will encourage you to add mulch later.

Many container gardens need about five hours of daylight. For vegetables, root vegetables require more water, while leafy vegetables need less sunlight. Vegetables bearing fruits like tomatoes need full sunshine. Use a low liquid fertilizer while watering your container garden plants. Potting mixtures drain very easily, and if you apply fertilizer as in a normal garden, it continues to drain. Water the plants regularly during the summer months as container plants loose moisture very quickly.

How to Plan Your Container Garden

The first thing to consider when planning a container garden is whether you'd rather grow your plants indoors or outdoors. Many people think container gardening is for indoor growing and patios, but containers can be useful for any garden situation.

Containers are perfect for growing almost any plant type, as they offer great flexibility. If you plant your garden in containers and need to move it later, it's quick. Not if you have got a conventional garden!

If you expect really bad weather, you may temporarily move containers to a safer spot, like indoors, garage or basement. But you can't do anything with a conventional garden.

If you notice your plants are not doing well because the room you want is too sunny or too dark, you can't do anything with a conventional garden, but you can easily switch potted plants to a better spot.

If you want to have your container garden outside, select a suitable place for it. You'll want to pick a location that has the right amount of sun for the plants you want to grow, but it's also a location that's very open. When working on your garden, it's easy to lose energy if it's several hundred yards from the house!

Place your plants as far from the streets as you can. Car emissions and the dust they kick up will harm and contaminate your plants. You don't want to consume all that waste, so find plants as far from those roads as possible.

If you have your plants indoors, you'll need to pick a really good spot. Most plants must be relatively dry, so if you use air conditioning, you'll need to pick the warmest spot in your building.

Most plants won't do well in very cold homes, so you might need to choose a space for your plants and keep the vent closed in that room to keep it cooler. If you can, choose a bright space with natural sunlight.

Plants flourish with natural light. If you don't have space with plenty of sunshine, use special plant lights for your plants. You can't use any fluorescent lighting as plants won't survive.

You need lights specially designed to grow plants. They provide a broad light spectrum, closer to natural light than regular bulbs. You may also need to change the room humidity with your plants.

Some plants perform best in higher humidity, some in lower humidity. If you raise very fragile or picky plants, you may need to invest in special equipment to change humidity. You probably won't have to do this without developing exotic varieties.

Ultimately, decide whether to organically cultivate your plants. If you're growing indoors, it'll probably be very easy. But if you cultivate your plants outside, the stress of dealing with pests is just too much for you. Don't feel bad if organic gardening is too difficult. You should still try after more practice.

There are thousands of containers for planting. Depending on your budget, certain plants are better than others, and it depends on how you want your garden to look. There are many things to consider when buying containers for your garden.

Once fully grown, the most important thing to consider is how much space your plants will need. Transplanting a near-full-grown plant will shock it seriously enough to die. Ensure the container has sufficient drainage. You don't want your plants to sink by mistake or rain from overwatering. If you cultivate edible plants, make sure the material isn't poisonous to people (or animals). This can be a wood-treated problem.

You may want to consider positioning them on a wheeled platform or dolly for large containers, and for easier travel. So you can push your big plants quickly and easily to take advantage of the sun or keep them out of the heat.

Most household products can be recycled to plant containers to save money and benefit the ecosystem. This can make a special, sexy look, depending on what you're using. Include cut-off milk jugs, detergent jugs, styrofoam containers and coolers, cinder blocks, drainage pipe and everything else around the building. Decorate your home-made containers with paints, permanent markers, ribbons or whatever you want. Know that containers have a lot to do with your container garden's attractiveness.

CHAPTER SIX
Fruit and Vegetables in Pots

Growing your own vegetables and aromatic herbs is tempting, especially when the weather is good. Who doesn't want to go for a walk in their garden and pick the day's juicy vegetables to make their meal? Unfortunately, if you don't have a small garden well known as a vegetable garden or worse if you don't have a garden at all, then the vision ends there.

It is here the planters come in. A large number of valued, edible plants are growing in pots. So wherever you want you can put them: in a garden, on a terrace or even on a balcony.

Please note that there are a few basic rules to follow. Next, your planter needs to be the right size to fit the plant you have selected. Lettuces, spinach, and aromatic herbs need little space. By contras, the tomatoes and peppers are round, yes.

Many basic rules: the use of "special edible plants in containers" for potting soil encourages plant growth in the planter. The garden soil should be avoided because it is too thick. You should also know that watering frequency is more critical in pot-growing than in a patch of vegetables. Indeed, as is the case in open land, the roots won't have the possibility to leave the pot to receive water.

Finally, if you put the plants on a balcony, make sure it supports the weight, and no condominium regulations forbid the planting! Small containers are typically not a problem, but it would be a shame if your laurel planter fell onto the patio below your neighbor.

If you want 100% organic fruits and vegetables, you can choose to have your own greenhouse. You can have complete control over what goes into an increasing phase. You can, for example, avoid using chemically rich composts and fertilizers and use organic ones.

A big factor in growing your own fruits and vegetables is the place you want to plant them. Choosing a spot where there's plenty of sunshine is always important. While different temperature zones exist, each zone has its own unique range to expand. Yes, as long as you do things right while you work, you will be able to produce your own organic goods.

Typically, growing vegetables in a pot are done on the balcony. However, in order to realize this idea, you need to comply with the requirements of the plants and the exposure of the balcony. If it is shaded for most of the day, you cannot grow a light-loving plant, even if the exposure is south. So take a close look at the requirements of the vegetables we present to you and decide what to grow on your terrace.

Space is not a limitation for growing fruits and vegetables

You can have a big garden or a small plot. Even you could live in a garden-free flat or home. There are several different gardening techniques and methods that allow you to do almost anywhere.

For example, container gardening allows you to grow fruits and vegetables in a small greenhouse, patio and balcony. These containers can easily grow dwarf fruit trees. Tomatoes, cucumbers, onions and herbs can be cultivated in small containers.

Here are some advantages of container gardening:

- Besides helping you to grow your own organic vegies and fruits, they can also be a good decorative device. Imagine getting a dwarf apple tree on your tiny patio, full of apples. How cool and stunning to the eyes.
- They can be easily handled and maintained. With your garden in a large pot, you don't have to worry about high maintenance jobs to keep your garden clean.
- They're very mobile, a big benefit. You can quickly change your container garden's location if it doesn't get enough sunlight. If you ever move to another town, you can take it with you.

So, whether you stay in a large garden house or in a flat with no garden at all, different gardening approaches will match your circumstances. You can cultivate your own organic fruit and vegetables.

Ten easy-to-grow fruit and vegetable varieties in pots

- **Aromatic herbs**

Herbs are pleasant in pots of all sizes, placed on a window sill or along an aisle. For herbs of the mint family, it is strongly advised to plant them in a planter if you do not want your garden to be completely invaded in the years to come.

The trick to planting potted herbs is to choose containers that can accommodate the adult plant. Smaller herbs such as chervil, chives, cilantro, marjoram, oregano, parsley, sage, savory, tarragon and thyme can be grown in planters 15 to 30 cm deep and 30 cm maximum width. Basil, lavender and lemongrass will work best in pots of 40 to 45 cm minimum and rosemary and dill in larger planters. As for the bay leaf, start with a 45 cm pot before replanting it in the garden, or prune it to control its growth.

- **Salads**

Salads are also easy to grow in pots since most varieties have shallow roots. Placing them in a raised container like an old wheelbarrow allows them to be highlighted rather than ignored, as is often the case with plants that grow on the ground. You can only plant one type of salad per pot or mix it up. You will need a pot 15 cm deep for most lettuces, mixed greens and green vegetables, as well as 20 cm for endives, chicory and spinach.

- **Strawberries**

What a pleasure to see your strawberries growing and watching the stems grow heavy under the weight of the fruit! By placing them in pots, you can put them wherever you want and pick some for a gourmet break in your garden or on your terrace. And why not grow your strawberries in a hanging pot? This will have the advantage of keeping snails and slugs away. A strawberry planter is a must, and strawberries are not difficult to grow. It is enough to place them in a depth of soil of at least 20 centimeters. If you plant them in a hanging basket, opt for a larger pot with a width and a depth of about 30 centimeters.

The strawberry delight especially well in pots and in the sun. The advantage is that once planted, and they give beautiful fruits every year without taking care of them. You can vary the early and late varieties to have them throughout the summer.

Figure 5 - Strawberries

Easy to plant because they require neither a lot of space nor a lot of maintenance, and adapt perfectly to the culture in the pot on a balcony. Strawberries and raspberries are ideal to be grown on the edge of a window. Plant the feet of strawberries or raspberries in a pot about 30 cm in diameter and depth. Fill the pot with potting soil on a background lined with gravel or shards. Place the tray of strawberries and raspberries in full sun. Water regularly to keep the soil slightly moist.

- **Peppers**

Although pepper is a vegetable that grows very well in a vegetable patch, sowing in a pot will allow you to start growing earlier. You sow them in pots placed in a protected place, and then you can replant them in your vegetable patch, where they will take advantage of the heat of summer to ripen. The only problem with peppers grown in planters is that they rarely reach the size of vegetables planted in a vegetable patch. But they remain just as tasty and will bring wonderful touches of color to your balcony or patio. Your planter should be at least 20 cm deep (30 cm deep is optimal) and be 40 to 45 cm wide.

Peppers have a great pot yield and have no problem growing in a small space. They just need sun and warmth. A pot at least 30 cm deep, soil drained with a little fertilizer at the time of planting, and voila.

- **Tomatoes**

Tomatoes planted in pots are just as tasty as tomatoes in the ground. This type of culture also has an advantage if you live in an area where there are soil-borne plant diseases. Plant your tomatoes in pots and renew the soil every year, so you won't have to worry about the rotation of your crops. Once you have found the ideal location for your tomatoes, you can place them in the same place from one year to the next.

As with other edible plants, you will need to make sure your planter matches the size of your adult tomato plants. My advice is to think big, because even small cherry tomatoes will need a pot or hanging basket at least 30 centimeters deep and wide, while varieties of large tomatoes will need to be planted in a pot. Although the sight of the branches of tomatoes overflowing from your planter is a real pleasure for the eyes, it is recommended to provide stakes for varieties of large tomatoes.

For their normal development require 18-30 degrees. If the temperature is below 15 degrees, flowering stops. Due to the heat above 30 degrees, the leaves remain small, and the branches of the stems thin. It is possible to drop the colors. At below 15 and above 40 degrees, no dye is formed, and the fruits turn yellowish. High temperatures cause sunburn on the fruit if the leaves do not shade them. If the terrace is shady, your tomatoes will not rise, they love the sun. Vegetables need moisture - the soil moisture should be above 70-80% and 50-60% air. Tomatoes are demanding on the soil. Their root system develops deep, so prepare a large pot (maybe a tin of cheese, but it won't be pretty). Fill it with nutrient-rich soil mix: two parts of well-burned manure and one part of the soil. Consider your balcony options and plant tomatoes. Regularly water and nourish with sherbet.

- **Eggplants**

Eggplants are often overlooked in vegetable gardens and planters adorning modern balconies. It's a shame because the plant is beautiful and offers beautiful purple flowers in spring, then sparkling fruits of purple (which come in variations of white, green, red and yellow). Eggplants are not very large but need room to grow well. Choose a planter about 30 cm deep and 40 to 45 cm wide, then give it a place of honor among your other pots.

- **Potatoes**

If you make a list of plants suitable for planting in pots, potatoes will certainly be absent. A potato planter is, however, quite feasible as long as you opt for a container that is large enough, such as a barrel cut in half, for example. The procedure: rather than burying your potatoes to the desired depth, plant shallowly, then add potting soil as the tubers grow. Planting them in a barrel makes this easier. And while the tubers are growing, you can still admire and benefit from the green plant with its pale-colored flowers.

- **Zucchini**

Summer squash, especially compact varieties like this patisson, can be controlled in terms of their size when grown in pots. Thus, you will no longer have to search under kilometers of oversized leaves to find your zucchini, not easily visible unless they reach the size of Godzilla. Another piece of advice: prefer non-staked varieties rather than climbing plants, unless you want to set up a trellis. Either way, you won't be able to get by with tiny pots facing these high-growing plants. Opt for a pot of 45 cm in diameter for each zucchini plant, or even larger.

Very easy to grow, they have the advantage of having rapid growth and very pretty flowers. Plant zucchini in a tray PVC or metal of at least 60 cm in diameter. Fill it with soil rich in organic matter. Place in full sun sheltered from the wind and water regularly.

The zucchini delight pot and are easier to maintain than squash. It is one of the easiest vegetables to grow in pots on a balcony or patio. They will give you generous and abundant fruit if they are in full sun. Choose a variety of "non-runner"and with small fruits like the "round of Nice."

Very easy to grow, they have the advantage of having rapid growth and very pretty flowers. Plant zucchini in a tray PVC or metal of at least 60 cm in diameter. Fill it with soil rich in organic matter. Place in full sun sheltered from the wind and water regularly.

- **Dwarf beans**

Technically, the most common variety of snap beans can grow in a planter, but dwarf beans are better choices because they are smaller. There are many varieties. Look for rather large containers, but be aware that if you only have a depth of 15 centimeters, this will not prevent the success of your harvest. If you opt for climbing beans, add stakes when planting. Beans can be grown in pots but require a pan large and deep (40 cm minimum) because it produces many fine roots. Plant your beans in a compost garden light and well-drained so that the roots do not rot. Green beans blossomed quickly alongside strawberries, carrots, cabbage and cucumbers. Do not hesitate to involve them in one large bin.

- **Lemons**

Figure 6- Lemon tree

You may live in a region where the winters are cold, but rest assured, this will not prevent you from growing your own lemons or limes, oranges or kumquats. You will just have to make sure to plant them in a pot exposed to outside light in summer, and placed in a shelter or in your house in winter. You can start with a fairly small pot when your tree is young, but be aware that you will then have to replant it in a larger pot at least 45 centimeters deep and wide. To be able to move the pot, place it on a roller base. You will be able to make your own citrus juice, even if you live in Dunkirk.

- **Cucumbers - on the northeast terrace**

The cucumber is very heat-loving and water-loving. Plants grow well at 25-30 degrees Celsius and high humidity of 90%. At below 15 degrees, growth stops. It is slightly demanding of light and develops relatively well when shaded.

The root system is weak and superficial, so you should water it regularly. Drought during flowering and flopping adds color and knotting, and the cucumbers are deformed. Low soil and air humidity make them bitter. Vegetables are extremely demanding on soil and air humidity. Prepare the fertilizer-soil mixture, fill it in chests and sow the seeds in a radish 10-15 cm distance and 3-4 cm deep. Regularly water and nourish with sherbet. A warm northeast balcony with more watering and nourishment will reward you with fresh vegetables for your favorite tarator.

- **Lettuce**

The lettuce grows very quickly, thereby is often harvested throughout the season. In general, it is sown in the spring, but beware, it fears frost. So, depending on your region, wait for the right time to sow it. To grow it, you need a large but shallow pot. Leave a space of about 10 cm between each future salad. Depending on the lettuce varieties, they take up more or less space. For example, the "Appia" lettuce produces a large head while the "Sloth" spreads with large green leaves. Always keep the soil moist and well-drained.

- **Radishes**

The radishes are really suitable for pot culture. In addition, in 3 weeks, the harvest is already there. You can grow them in pots of any size. 15 cm deep is enough, or more if you can, but remember to leave them a little space between them.

- **Shanghai Cabbage**

Shanghai cabbage is perfectly suited for growing in pots because it is not bulky. In addition, it does not need a lot of suns: the morning sun is enough (about 3 hours a day). Consider putting natural fertilizer on them regularly and keeping the soil moist.

- **Kale**

The kale is perfectly suited to container culture. Harvest the young leaves at once, or let it grow and harvest it several times. Kale likes cool places, and it becomes bitter in hot weather. Depending on your region, plant it in the sun (for cool regions) and in a semi-shaded area (warm region).

- **Mustard greens**

The mustard greens like heat and have an advantage: they require no care. Put them in a medium pot, in full sun. Choose the variety of mustard you prefer: the "Dragon Tongue" is purplish and rather sweet, while the "Green wave" is strong and spicy. Choose the large leaves for cooking in curry, and the young shoots for salads.

- **Garlic**

The garlic bulbs are quite expensive, but they have so many health benefits that we should not do without. And then, growing them yourself in pots is very economical. You can cook the bulbs, but also the leaves in salads. Choose a pot at least 20 cm deep and wide enough to leave 15 cm between each bulb.

CHAPTER SEVEN
Vertical Planting System

The vertical vegetable garden is the answer to growing vegetables in a small space. The idea was born especially for those who live in the city and do not have a plot of land but only a small garden, if not simply a little space on the terrace or balcony. Those in these conditions are normally forced to give up the pleasure of growing their favorite vegetables, putting aside their green thumb and the idea of bringing something self-produced to the table.

Fortunately, these people come across the vertical vegetable garden, which, as the name suggests, takes advantage of the vertical space by arranging the containers with the sowing in height on different shelves. Obviously, there are some rules to follow, and you can't just stack the pots at random.

Another excellent idea, if you have space, includes running a partition right to the fence. This gives more plant-growing surfaces. Cover certain surfaces with wire or trellises, using planting boxes for root crops on other surfaces.

You won't need a large plot for trellis vegetable gardening. Even if you just have a walkway and fence, in planters, you can cultivate some plants, or anywhere you can build a trellis. If you have room, use the ground for root crops such as beets and carrots, and as I said, grow wine on trellises or fences or walls.

Don't push the first year too hard. Put in a few crops and enjoy trellis planting, rather than attempting to grow so many vegetables that planting becomes a chore. You can grow vegetables parallel to fences or walls directly in the ground wherever you can install a trellis-or use planter.

How you do depends on the area's room and character. If I have a patio, gardening in containers is far easier. When you grow other plants in a small garden area, growing in the ground with trellis support will harmonize better with the overall scheme.

You can also expand flower gardens vertically. You can grow fruit trees with great success vertically. Most berries are climbers and thus suitable for vertical gardening.

Types of vertical gardening

There are different options for growing a vertical garden. Here's what they are:

1. Growth in a vertical container

You can buy or buy vertical container gardens. If you want to create your own, you need to create a frame with slats.

From there, you will see large windows that will easily attach to the frame. You can plant and grow vertically very easily.

Although you can also use a similar configuration for the sake of simplicity.

In both cases, the containers offer you the possibility of growing a variety of vegetables in a compact manner.

2. Pocket Gardening

You can create your own canvas pocket garden with a fabric canvas. You sew pockets into the canvas pocket, or you can use it for the sake of simplicity.

However, you can also buy one.

Either way, landscaped gardens allow those who have no room for growth to be able to grow something, provided they have a sunny wall.

3. wall planters

Wall planters are basic planters that attach to a wall and make it easier to grow different varieties of flowers or vegetables.

Again, it's easy to grow vegetables when you don't have a growing space, but rather a balcony wall or a divider between living spaces in urban areas.

4. Pallet planter

is an inexpensive way to grow a vertical garden. There are several ways to convert a pallet to a planter.

However, I used a palette to grow a herb garden. I used old jugs of milk and hung them on the pallet with the handle of the pitcher. It was inexpensive and simple to create.

5. shelves

is a great option for a vertical garden because it expands your horizons. You can plant a container garden and put all the containers on the shelf.

It will be easier to plant more varieties of vegetables in a compact space.

6. Hanging basket

are another great way to broaden your horizons with vertical gardening. You can grow tomatoes and other fruit plants that would otherwise be hard to grow in a pocket on a wall.

7. trellis

Finally, you can wall. A trellis wall will facilitate the cultivation of vegetables with long vines such as cucumbers or green beans. The trellis will allow the plants to grow instead of going out. This facilitates their growth in a compact space.

How to grow a vertical garden

Growing a vertical garden is more complicated than other varieties of gardening. The reason is that plants should be encouraged to grow differently from what they usually are. That said, here is what you need to know to grow your own vertical garden:

1. Where will he go?

The advantage of a vertical garden is that it can go anywhere. You can grow it outside on a balcony or a separation wall.

You can also grow a vertical garden indoors.

But you can also grow a vertical garden that goes outside when it's hot and indoors when it's cold. You will need to find a way to wheel your vertical garden or make it easy to move from base to base.

Again, if you want a vertical hybrid garden, using shelving is the easiest and probably the cheapest method.

2. Choose your plants

There are a few important options that you need to consider when deciding what to plant in your vertical garden.

First, you will need to choose flexible plants. If you choose plants, such as dwarf fruit trees or blueberries to place in a vertical garden, they branch out.

This will make your vertical garden spread out over the verses. This defies the whole purpose of your garden being compact.

In short, you need to choose plants that will flow easily (especially if you are creating a garden with vertical pockets).

Naturally, your options open up if you decide to use shelves with containers or hanging baskets.

Then you need to choose plants that have similar needs. You usually don't have the ease of moving vertical gardens.

With this in mind, you need to plant vegetation that can withstand full sun or needs a lot of shade.

3. Good soil is a must

As you plant vegetables in an area other than the soil, they will not have the opportunity to draw nutrients from a large amount of soil around them.

In fact, they will have very little land around them. This is why it is essential to use quality potting soil when planting your vegetables.

4. Start your plants

Then you have to go somewhere other than the vertical garden. A vertical garden has a gravity that always pulls on it. This makes it difficult to develop healthy roots.

For this reason, you should start your plants indoors until they are in full bloom. When the plants are vigorous, you can plant them in the vertical garden.

At this point, they should be able to manage gravity by pulling on them as they grow.

5. water frequently

You should be sure of yourself. Plants have shallow roots due to limited growing space.

Also, they don't have much soil to help them retain moisture. These two factors make it difficult for a plant to retain water indefinitely.

Water is a great way to water a vertical garden that sits on a wall, such as a folding garden.

6. Need for fertilizer

Plants growing in a vertical garden cannot get nutrients from the soil around them because they are not planted in the soil.

With that in mind, realize that your plants will have to be. This will give them the nutrients they need to thrive. You can feed them by hand with a liquid fertilizer in a sprayer or include them in the irrigation system when watering.

7. Plant insurance

Finally, you will need to keep adding plants on hand, as some plants will die in a vertical garden. This happens because plants have a shallow root system.

However, when the plants in your vertical garden begin to die, their appeal is less attractive. It is a good idea to grow additional plants and keep them in other containers.

This way, when a plant dies, you can extract the dead and put a healthy one back in the vertical paradise of your vegetable patch.

Benefits of the vertical garden

Before finishing, we would like to talk to you about some of the advantages of installing a vertical garden in your house. Take note!

- It starts you on self-consumption: this way you will know where the food you eat comes from and you will start to have a much more natural diet.
- It unites you as a family: because you can organize new activities, both planting and creating more space.

- It is a very healthy activity: it not only stimulates your imagination, but also allows you to exercise outdoors and stay active.
-

Vertical Gardening With Vegetables

A vertical garden is a method of cultivation above ground, which allows growing vegetables, and plants in general, stage by stage. The principle is to be able to cultivate everywhere, without necessarily having space on the ground, as long as you benefit from correct sunshine and a little water.

Unlike a horizontal vegetable patch, the vertical vegetable patch allows you to produce as much or even more over a smaller area. The culture can be done in soil or in an inert substrate (sand, clay balls). It is possible to have a vertical vegetable garden for a few euros for a simple system, and a few hundred euros for larger and automated systems.

The vertical vegetable garden is often done outside, but can very well be set up inside in an apartment, as long as you have a bright window. The small footprint and the ease of cultivation make it a real trend for years to come. Produce at home, anywhere, without space, just with the desire to eat vegetables and aromatics "from the garden".

VERTICAL GARDENING is tested to grow vegetables. If you have a clear understanding of vertical gardening concepts and the few criteria vegetables really need to grow, you're more likely to have a good experience with your vertical garden.

Root Space Is Key

Usually, vertical gardens have more limited root space than those on the ground, so find a system that has plenty of root room for your vegetables and you'll be off to a great start. If you've ever grown vegetables in containers, you'll know how critical it is to keep soil temperatures and moisture levels as even as possible. Plants that are stressed of heat or water quickly lose vigor; in these conditions, vegetables often 'rocket' to seed, resulting in very low growth.

Triple Your Existing Growing Space

Yeah, yeah ... The use of a soil-based, vertical garden system is a perfect option for space-restricted gardeners. Growing a large pot garden takes up plenty of floor space. Vertical garden systems actually build planting space; you can triple your area's square meter by going vertically and harvesting abundantly!

No Pots - No Trays!

Compared to pots and many other vertical gardening systems, soil volumes in steel vertical systems are massive. In this vertical gardening method, plant roots can move over half a cubic meter of soil media thickness. This large volume of soil helps greatly maintain even temperatures and humidity levels, thussaving time and energy compared to other vertical gardening systems and other planters.

Looking Good

Your vegetables excel in this vertical garden system, but they also look stunning. Your vertical garden will become a feature in any space; a living green wall that embellishes and feeds the whole family! In restricted areas, aesthetics are so critical, but everybody deserves fresh salad!

Feeding Tips

Thanks to the wide body of soil media in the open tiered, steel vertical gardening method, plants may benefit from a wide nutrient supply. Regular feeding with conventional watering liquid fertilizers and some slow release fertilizer a few times a year, is all that is required.

No Moving Parts

Many vertical gardening systems are focused on hydroponic growing methods where plants are anchored to matting or foam and have additional systems to monitor irrigation and fertilizer solution applications; however, the open tiered, steel vertical gardening system is based on a conventional low-tech gardening experience. This vertical garden is lined with soil media (potting mix) from top to bottom, and basically you only plant your favorite vegetable seeds or seedlings with your trowel into the exposed potting media and water them in. Water your vertical garden with collected rain or mains water with any tool you want, such as watering pipe, hose or automatic dripper system.

Vertical Gardening With Herbs

Like vegetables, herbs also like moisture and temperature levels, so building a broad root mass is essential to your success, and vertical gardening is the perfect solution. Herbs love growing in vertical gardens with a quality potting mix rather than felt or foam types of green walls; so herbs react very well in an open, steel vertical gardening system. Moreover, due to the increased root space available compared to conventional planting methods, many gardeners find that in the open tiered, steel vertical gardening system, herbs perform better than they ever have in pots!

The varieties of herbs you select in a vertical garden will depend on your tastes and appearance. For Asian herbs, select coriander, lemongrass and mint. Maybe your kitchen is more Italian, and you want to grow garlic, basil and oregano. It should be remembered that some herbs are perennial, and last year for a year, others are annuals or biennials, and will have to be replaced annually by seeds or cuttings. Regardless of the transplanting method you choose, an open-layer vertical steel gardening system is suitable as you simply grow your garden in a potting mix-as usual. Perhaps using smaller plants or seeds is cheaper, so you'll save time by having fun growing your own plants from scratch.

If you have little water available in your vertical garden, plant the tougher Mediterranean style herbs like curry plant, rosemary, sage, oregano and thymes. Whether your vertical garden has more security and/or water storage, you can also plant the slightly more delicate herbs like coriander, basil, parsley.

Some herbs are so vigorous, they will overwhelm the tenderer varieties in your vertical garden. Be warned that planting in the mint family or lemon balm is likely to spread and drown the other herbs in your vertical garden.

Whether in a vertical garden or not, herbs love daily picking to encourage fresh, flavorful, tip production. The more you choose, the more you get; so even if you don't want to eat herbs, prune frequently to keep plants healthy and ample supply.

Use rainwater or water to keep your soil-based, open tiered, vertical garden in good shape. Either hand water as needed, or use a simple automated dripper device to take care of watering when away or forgetting.

Vertical herb gardening is deliciously simple, a wonderful activity to share with grandchildren and give you an attractive, aromatic, year-round abundance of culinary joy! After you've tasted the difference, dried stuff will never return to the musty 'past use by date.'

CHAPTER EIGHT
Raised Bed Gardening

If you enjoy eating fresh organic vegetables but don't like pulling weeds or running up a big water bill with a conventional row garden, then you'll enjoy square foot gardening. Square foot gardening is performed in a 4-foot garden bed consisting of four side panels and no edge. You'll need a weed barrier to build the edge. Instead you fill the bed with a special soil mix: three equal parts of vermiculite (to retain moisture), peat moss (to make the soil light and drain loose), and compost (for nutrients). You can find these in your nearest nursery or garden shop. If you're eager to get started right away, just buy the commercial compost now. But it will do well to start making your own organic compost later. It's a smart way to use your kitchen vegetable scraps and lawn clippings as well as save money on industrial fertilizer.

Raised bed gardening, square foot gardening is often named. The original idea was to increase the gardens' growth and yield. This form of plantation often decreases the use of water and is a perfect way to grow a garden in low soil areas.

You start by building a simple four-foot-square raised bed. A bed of this size makes it easy from either side to reach the middle. Use timber eight to 12 inches generally, so your bed is lifted tall. Put the fresh ground in the house. You're going to want to add some fertilizer slow down. It feeds your plants in the summer and helps increase your crop growth.

You can plant your raised bed in many ways. You can divide the bed by string in a foot by a foot. This gives you nine equal spaces for development. This portion is suitable for small crops such as onions, herbs and so on. You will only want one or two plants per segment if you grow plants that have bigger plants, such as tomatoes.

Another alternative is to split the bed evenly into two. It's a perfect way to grow corn, beans and potatoes. Wide spreading crops such as tomatoes, pumpkins, and watermelons will each need their own bed so they have room to spread.

When planting your fields, consider how big every plant eventually gets. You don't want smaller plants like corn shading. Keep your plants grouped big to tiny, and plant north to south.

This method of planting allows plants to grow closer together, growing the space that weeds need to grow. Near planting also tends to shade the soil, retaining moisture longer and helping to conserve water. The plants are well fertilized from the slow-release fertilizer you first mixed in the soil, and they have enough water. They also get plenty of light by paying attention to their size when planting.]

Reasons To Consider Building A Raised Bed Garden

Perfect Soil

There is a raised garden above your current level of soil where you fill the soil you want. Then, you can get the exact perfect soil your plants need to grow and make sure it's perfectly balanced, so your plants get the best chance for lush growth.

Better Drainage

Since the soil you place in your raised bed is looser than the natural soil in your backyard, the raised garden has much more drainage than the majority of gardens. Drainage is necessary to successfully grow plants since most plants can not grow in standing water.

Higher Yield

If you want to grow more plants in the same room, it's a great way to create a raised bed garden. You can plant the plants in a raised garden closer together because the beds are designed so that you don't have to enter between the plants for maintenance. Closer growth of the plants means more plants per square foot.

Easy Maintenance

Raised bed gardens are easier to maintain as every floor in the bed can easily be reached. The idea was to build your bed so that it doesn't have a limit of 4 feet long at any point and then point it at least 2 feet away if you have more than one bed. So you can easily touch any plant from outside the bed and you have an aisle to go in, without having to go into the bed to plumb, harvest or care for your plants otherwise. It also makes weeding and putting down mulch much easier.

Less Soil Compaction

Since the raised bed is easier to maintain and doesn't allow you to walk through the rows of plants for maintenance, soil compaction should be much less meaning, so that the plants have more growth opportunities and fewer break-up opportunities.

Creating a raised bed garden isn't that difficult. What you need is some kind of material to make the 4 sides, and you can use boards or specially-made beds that you can buy in the garden shop. A raised garden can be any height, but make sure yours is at least 6 inches off the ground.

Some people now use very large waistbands that allow them to grow plants very easily, and if you are able to plant them all standing, it is much easier on their knees. Such elevated gardens are ideal for both vegetables and flowers, and are a perfect way to add height and scale to your landscape.

Advantages of Raised Beds Gardening

Gardening on raised beds provides some important advantages over conventional agriculture, which allows it to be used to grow ornamental plants and naturally, vegetables for many years. Raised beds help to resolve unadapted soils and terrain, and provide a way for people with back and knee issues to start gardening.

When designing our plant garden we look for three important requirements in the garden: plenty of sunshine, good soil and good drainage; and of course, a rich supply of water. Although we can place our garden to full sunlight every day, the consistency of the soil can not always be managed, and unsuitable land can be costly and not necessarily practical. Here, lifted beds can solve most of our difficulties.

If the soil is founded on clay and very firm and has low drainage in the only place you need, a raised bed alleviates the problem that the water is slowly draining through the bed. A slight excavation full of gravel or coarse rocks can help with drainage problems if your only option is the boggy water field. Building high-rise beds on steep slopes is a good way to use wasted space and beds often avoid sloping erosion using the runoff in your beds.

Raised beds allow you to maximize room for cultivation because rows are removed, and you can still reach the plants on the back when making beds up to four feet deep. This gardening method allows a greater number of plants to be grown than a traditional garden allows, and helps to control weeds due to the shade of good plants.

Raised garden beds can be made from old lumber or railway sleepers found or bought; should be at least about 12 inches tall and can be made up to waist height if materials allow or if you have back or knee problems. For the selfish gardener with a weak back, raised beds will keep them doing what they enjoy. If the stakes are driven into the ground to support them, old fence palings or floor boards can also be used.

Very little ground preparation is needed before the bed is built; the grass is managed by a few layers of ancient press and if the ground is 12-inch deeper or larger, the field may shock the grass before reaching the surface. A high stake in every corner stops the plants from damaging when the pants are pulled over your pillow.

The raised beds should warm up much more quickly in the spring and dry up quickly after heavy rain; this ensures optimal plant growth conditions. The only downside with raised beds is that in extremely hot weather, they can dry up faster and need to be watered more often. For portable shade cloth coverings, this can be minimized even on particularly hot days.

Planting is still a popular hobby for both families and couples, but smaller lots or no lots have sparked interest in raised bed planting. This famous gardening method enables the cultivation of fresh fruit and vegetables in small areas, just a few meters away. As knowledge of eating grows locally, locals spread the word; a small amount of fresh food grows in a small plot.

Soil dispersed over ground heats up more rapidly in the spring, which allows for better seeding opportunities. Most gardeners face challenging conditions in the soil. Heavy clay or light sandy soils are rising under conditions that even the most experienced gardener is frustrated. Raised bed planting allows the grower to blend the recet for optimal growth with the best ingredients. Top land, compost, mouths and nutrients allow healthy plants to grow on denser plantings that reduce the inflammation of weeds.

Garden size depends on how much raised bed planting you want to do. Keeping the bed four feet wide allows easy access from both sides. A six-to-eight-inch bed depth is suggested because most of the major feeder roots are at this depth. Locate the bed in full sun if possible; if not, at least half a day of sunlight is required for good plant growth. A water supply should be nearby, as raised bed gardens dry out faster than traditional gardening.

CONCLUSION

If you're among that number of people who want to turn to container gardening, then you're right. There's plenty of useful information on this new form of gardening here.

Millions worldwide are seeking container gardening these days. With its many advantages, nothing comes as a surprise. Indeed, many wonder why they haven't tried it years ago.

One of the key advantages of this style of gardening is that you don't need a sprawling garden to try. Since all plants will be planted in containers, you can build it according to any room available in your home. Additionally, you can also arrange and then rearrange the containers to fit them with your house's interiors.

Container gardening is popular for another cause, accessibility. For starters, plants are easier for the elderly. They can touch and tend plants quickly. Via this special yet realistic idea, disabled people can also enjoy their share of gardening.

Soil quality is another reason many seek container gardening. Since you can grow plants in containers, you can always ensure good soil quality. It's not always that you grow plants in a traditional garden. Additionally, you also have the option to change the soil with the containers if at any time you feel the quality is not good and substitute it at your convenience.

With plants growing in a container feeding them, it is much simpler. You can easily use fertilizers and live with plants. It also means that the fertilizer or pesticide you use is not wasted and benefits the plants.

If you grow plants in a greenhouse, you always experience an extended growing season. You're no longer at the mercy of the environment, and you can seek to cultivate different plants easily from the comforts of your home. With so many benefits, container gardening is finding an increasing number of takers these days.

www.ingramcontent.com/pod-product-compliance
Lightning Source LLC
Chambersburg PA
CBHW070920080526
44589CB00013B/1376